Heartbeats

Utkarsh Saurbh

The Heart of Heartbeats © 2023 Utkarsh Saurbh

Presentation by *BookLeaf Publishing*

Web: www.bookleafpub.com

E-mail: info@bookleafpub.com

ISBN:9789358730906

First edition 2023

DEDICATION

To all the souls out there.

The ones who are hurting.

The ones who have lost.

The ones who used to dream with open
eyes but now do not.

The ones who still have a dream.

The ones who forgot,

that they had a dream.

The ones who are lost.

The ones who are waiting,

to put in effort for their dreams.

The ones who try,

to live their life to the fullest,

and not just breathe and exist.

And the ones who are found.

I dedicate this volume of poetry to them.

May you find the courage, strength and drive to move past the obstacles in your life and make it big, as you should, and keep moving ahead to victories.

May you inspire others and keep inspiring.

May God and the universe bless you all.

ACKNOWLEDGEMENT

Eternal gratitude to my family, venerable teachers, dear friends and all the souls that have blessed me with their presence in my life. No man is an island and I'm no exception. I would have been nowhere without your care, love, company and guidance.

I would like to thank my teachers Manju Karnatak, Paul Mathew, Vinay Kumar Gupta, Praveen Shetty, Aneesha Acharya, Mukund Kumar Menon, Kapil Sadani, Nanditha Nair, Surekha Kamath and Ganesh Nayak. For everything.

Special thanks to my mentors Manisha Singh and Aabhas Sharma for their constant support, help and guidance. You two are just awesome.

Special thanks to my crazy friends, each of whom has filled my life with so many colours.

Manners maketh man. But so do the people in his life.

Many thanks to BookLeaf Publishing, my publisher, and Simi Tiwari, my editor.

PREFACE

Hey, you!

Yes, you, the amazing person who is reading this.

Thanks so much for picking up my book.

There is some stuff in here that I hope you would like and perhaps, even resonate with. The poems in this collection are based on my life in college and as a working professional. There is a range of deeply felt emotions here, feelings that deserved to adorn the paper, raging tempests that won't be quelled, my ups and downs and the states in between, with my warrior spirit trying to keep me steady through all that I have seen and felt and urging me to write.

You are a living being of infinite potential and are certainly a soul who loves artistic expression in some form or the other. I have tried to be honest in my poems and I feel it deep within that you would get me. Probably think of penning down your own thoughts, if you are not already. Think of dreaming of ambition and happiness and going after them, if you are not already.

Here's hoping my writings galvanise you into doing what you are absolutely passionate about. And find your calling, if you have not already.

Here is to your happiness and fulfilment.

Love,
Utkarsh

INDEX

One Dusk at a Time

Strewn across the azure in smoky wreaths,
The crimson clouds tremble and glide,
In a barely perceptible breeze.

Breathing inside the self-created grave,
Buried longings utter their sporadic screams,
Clamouring to be disinterred.

At last,
The somnolent sun gazes at me,
Illuminating the crevasse of my being,
Before plunging in the west.

To sleep.

The Heart of Heartbeats

Tiny, feeble, riffling thumps.
Thumping away beneath.
Stomping to their own beat.
Pre-chosen by them,
Or by someone else.

I don't know.
I don't get a say.

Tiny, feeble, ignored thumps.
Pressing softly in my eardrums.
Going about their work.
They don't share much.

I can't ask why.
I don't get to judge.

Signs of life.
Momentary, most important.
Must be working with quiet sneers.
They don't know rest.
Can't know a quiet moment.

Signatures of life.
Ever-present, never-dulled.
They make me feel they are,
When whipped by worthy emotions.

Proofs of life.
Will they survive my trenchant logics?
I don't think they care much.
I don't feel alive.

Baptism of Banishment

You become a night.
Simmering down.
Parched and pleading.
Stitched with the glint of stars.

Your eyes light up,
To the commotion within.
The deserted dream has beckoned you,
From the same old stars.

You sought the dream,
And breathed the flame.
Rummaged the past.
An incomplete lane.

That the dream was I,
You denied to know.
Furrowed your insouciance,
In knitted gelid brows.

And the pen you clasped,
Did pine for me.
Smothered in your silent sway,
Poured itself to let it be.

Solace I had wished for.
Did I welcome the bruise?
You discover me lying and fluttering,
Trembling in forsaken hope.
Crinkled and callused.

When the strands of thought,
Are smeared with blood and rain,
I awaken to the melody,
Of an impatient bane.

Then I am your redeemer.
Though not for long.
Mirth sails for your shores,
But it does not belong.

I watched the hewed desperation,
Floating all over me.
Sodden and seduced.

Freed seemed your shackled breath.
Startled and amused.

A hoary past sought you out.
And I did not care to see.
As you orphaned me in the tumult.
Crumpled and abused.

Control Freak

The dead of the night has dawned.
The sounds around me,
Have died down to a trickle.
Some dogs outside are awake.
Just like my fridge,
My clock,
My conscience,
And my ambitions.

The sounds weren't dead about an hour back.
And hours before that hour.
They were rushing by,
Keeping up with the time rushing by,
Keeping it company.
Or they were time itself.
I don't know for certain.

Now when I mention sounds,
I remember other things as well.
People and praises.
Articles and artists.
News and newsmakers.
Songs and songsters.
Sombre and whimsical scenes.
Deadlines and dead thoughts.

They too have rushed me by.
Like a madcap train rushing before your eyes.

How I would like to store and keep them,
In a folder of earthly dimensions?

All these mad things passing by.
Don't want to miss them.
Not even a single one.
Want to collect and hide them.
For myself.
Be they pleasing or otherwise.

But I can't find a folder of that size.
And even now it's zipping past.

Flying by.

Flying through.

Flying with me.

As for collecting and hiding,
I think my mind is the best bet.

Face Recovery Tool

A 'stranger' came to me in a dying dream,
Asking for my well-being.
His mannerisms told me I knew him.
From a long time ago.
A time when I had fewer alien faces around me.

Yet I wondered who the hell he was,
And why I couldn't recall his face.

After all, I knew him, right?

This was one of those dreams that you
remember,
Long after the night goes to sleep.
But the man went away with the night.
And didn't come back.
Leaving me chafing for moments.

But then I went back to work.
We all ultimately do.
Chafe when things slip away.
And then go back to work.

Sanity is invaluable.
Sanity is mighty important.
Not a bit of sarcasm to bite you.
Please try to understand.

Sometimes when work leaves me alone,
But very few times, trust me,
Your face floats up,
Taking me back,
Way back in the mists of memory.

And the odd question I then ask is:
"Have I remembered you,
In this list of vanishing faces?"

Nights of Waking Memories

Tonight,
Of today,
Will tell me a tale,
I couldn't hear in the day.

The day doesn't let me.
With all these people swarming around me.

Tonight,
Of today,
Will shove in a tale before my mind's eye,
The tale of a memory that got pushed back,
A memory that I'd forgotten,
And didn't even know had lost it,
Until tonight.

The tale spins in my mind.
The disquiet alarms.
I have to hear this.
This tale of a memory.
Of genial tempests and stormy quietudes.

Sometimes it's a single one.
Sometimes there are many.
Sometimes they clothe me in sadness.
Sometimes they are funny.

The night will come again,
I know.
I hope it brings a new memory.
And not the same old one.
Because I'd want to feel different tomorrow.

But I have little control over what's in store.

Or maybe the night's plan,
Is a string of memories.
To keep my mind alive.
Hoodwink slumber.
Give it food for thought.
Literally.

And on it will go.
Day by day.
A new night.
An old memory.
A fresh night.
A stale memory.

The moment I close my eyes for the day,
A story starts playing in my head.
A story without a beginning or an end.
A story I can't foretell.
A new one each day.
Composed of old and older memories.
That's how the nights roll for me.
Telling me the stories in my life.
Pricking me with my ambitions.
My failures and my wins.
My gains.
And my losses.
Is there a message here?
No.
I am just a bit more observant than you, I guess.

Disappearing Acts

It's high time I asked my memories,
How do they keep on stacking in my head,
Without some mechanism like a lock and key?
Is there a better way than that to stay safe?

Open my eyes to a new day,
And a few of them come stand by my side.
Some define the choices of the day.
Some define the days of my life.

I wish they could suggest a safehold.
Like chambers I could lock them into.
And open them any day I want.

Or requests I could send to them.
To come show themselves.
When they can't hear me,
In the din of thoughts.

Erratic and obstinate they could be.
Brain-mates with zero liabilities.
They come as they please.
I have little control.

Some of them stay back.
But as the seasons roll by,
Most of them end up scramming,
To hideouts only they know.

I am asking questions in the dead of the day.
All jumpy and stricken.
Questions I know won't get answered.
Gosh, I'll freak out if they were.
Then, I'll begin calling on a higher power for
assistance.
A higher power that was a stranger till now.

Warrior

And then came the rains,
Enervated with the ennui of the skirmishing
seasons.
They had promised to wash away the
bedraggling hurt,
That had seeped somewhere deep inside,
staining the breath of me.

And then sprung the pain,
That I had been saving for this opportune
moment.
A moment to sift through its own duration.
To take a pause in the scrimmage to make a
mark upon the world.
To refuse the will of the world and the chaos that
rules it.
To sweep away the traces of helplessness
brewing up inside.
To quell everything that smothered the already
latent vapid rages of hope.

Benumbed yet still aglow with the flickers of an
unequivocal vow.
To strip the soul from the clutches of an
unnamed fear,

To snatch the sickness adhering to the self,
And watch it getting ripped apart and floating
away.

I do not frolic in these moments always.
Though I want to but cannot choose to.
For it is a rarity to locate them,
In the multitude of impulses that ricochet
through the brain every day.
The birth of newer resolves and their eventual
defeatist slumber.
Lost almost daily in a haste for the elusive prize.

Not today.

Today they've failed to sneak by.
Balled shut in my fists that want to punch
through the walls of time.
It will be very long,
Before I let them slink away into oblivion again.

The rains have died down.
Inhaling the blessed memory of a freshened
future.
The waters have seeped somewhere deep inside.
Anointing the urge to bend the fortunes to my
will.

Satiated within the moistened folds of an
unrequited earth.

Urban Life

Boy, you're home!
Far away from the crowd and the noise.
So what if the day didn't go well?
You're now in the company of poise.

Sit back and relax.
Get that pint from the fridge and that smoke.
You think you've earned the silence,
That no one now can revoke.

The day is gone but is still afresh in you.
Save this mood for bedtime and morning too.
You're home, closer to you.
Like everyday in the night.

So sit back and relax.
In the bubble no one can poke.
Sip from the next pint you picked up,
In the curling wreaths of smoke.

Should you call someone?
Should you enthrall someone?
Could you troll someone?
Would you appall someone?
Or should you just lay down and do nothing,

Till the workplace of dreams takes over?

An iota of me-time before the drill begins afresh,
Is something that no one ever rues,
With winds of change perishing in a cold-press,
Lives here are defined by TVs that snooze.

The Songs in My Head

Uninterested in the pen.
Even in how I hold it.

How at times I want to put it away.
Yet it will write and scrawl.
Essentially dead but comes alive in my fingers.
Makes me crawl back to,
The songs inside my head.

I am a stocky, fearsome adult.
With proven records of bravery.
Yet I am sometimes terrified,
Of getting outside my head.
The world isn't what it used to be.
The world isn't what I thought it used to be.

I find I don't like all the songs.
But they live up there anyway.
Without permission or regards.
They know I can't ask them to leave.
I am a stocky, fearsome adult.
With proven records of bravery.

Days and months and years,
I find there are still some songs in my head,

That play in reverse and still are perfect,
Memorised through memories.
Not good or bad, but perfect.
Songs that don't top worldwide charts.
Songs that are written just for me.
By someone unknown to me.

There are still songs in my head.
A few I think were long dead.
But if they were really dead,
Why do I feel them probing me tonight?

Monsoon in Manipal

The fleecy clouds roll in,
Promising a hearty downpour.
Yellowed leaves float aloft,
The howling wind's roar.

The setting sun sets the west ablaze,
In scarlet and gold.
The last rays are yet to depart,
Shadows lengthen manifold.

The visitors reiterate their promise,
When distant rumble echoes softly.
Silver streaks cleave the firmament,
The parched earth waits expectantly.

The bewildering cacophony ensues,
Quaffing the essence of every sound.
Save for muffled cries of the soul,
Eerie stillness pervades profound.

Aliens Calling

Are you alone?
No, not in your life.
But in the grander scheme of things?

Things that may lie beyond your comprehension.
Things that may still lie obscured in your sight.

The most-evolved being on Earth.
Jiving to your own individual verse.
Master of none but your whims and fancies.
Usurper of the planet's resources.
Lording over other creatures.

But while confidence in oneself still tricks this
being,
In the supposed wilderness that we call the
universe,
Do you think in all those places beyond,
There exists a weird crop of creatures?

Are they friends with gentle minds?
Are they foes with cruel faces?
Or are they just another weathered race?
Striving to make their own residence a better
place?

You, mayhaps, are not interested yet.
Having had your fill of the Spielberg-created fear.
Caught up with your dreams and your fights all your life round.
But, there are mysteries still unsolved here,
And mysteries of the cosmos abound.

Oh, and they may not turn out as friends most humane.
The 'War of the Worlds' may still become a reality.
Then, what you will need is that 'most-evolved' brain.
Or the visitors will have your fealty.

"Either we are alone in the universe or we are not.
Both the eventualities are equally terrifying."
You may not be gung-ho about this thought,
But this was what Arthur Charles Clarke opined.

The Archived Loss

She is lit up,
With that unmistakable careless frown.
Aimed at the sleepy-eyed world.
A breathing alien world.

Or so he thinks.

She is lit up,
With the blackened intent of pain.
The remnants of her charred resolve,
Have huddled together to keep her sane.

And this he knows.

She is lit up,
With the yellowed glow in the dark.
As the balcony lamp overhead,
Bathes her face in an incandescence so stark.

She lifts up her face,
And catches his eyes.
A dream drunk clairvoyant she has transformed
into,
Predicting the perishing future.
While the light brown in her eyes,

Sprinkles the still of the vaunted night.

Then she averts her face,
From the probing threads of light.
Only to peer silently into the wet dark,
Drilled deep with the glinting bullets of light.

He is lit up,
With the fiery cherry glow of a Marlboro.
Sucking at the minute life,
That burned with the quest for burning
something else entirely.

He is lit up,
With a wordless jibe at his crude form.
A congealed core.
Solidified through the passage of time.

He has decided to brave the storm.

He now burns,
With the lamps of the night.
An unchangeable rictus,
He now burns up,
With the stealthy languid glow,
Eating him up insidiously inside.

His perspiring fingers,
Glistening in the embers of light,

Lift up to feel her black, wiry locks.
To find themselves caressing the cool in them,
And parting them gently
behind her ears.

Tangled his fingers had gotten.
He will remember too late.

He tickles her chin with his thumb,
To watch her blush,
And laugh her subdued laughter,
Which is still a crackle of joy.

How he wished to immure that moment in his
precious vault of memory.
To possess her and yet set her free.

Morjim

Staring out,
At this endless expanse roiling as the oceans,
Shimmering in the waning pride of the sun.

I'm at a loss with wounded reasons,
And yearning for at least one.

The waters grow adamant.
Numbing my body.
Stinging my soul.
Unforgiving to both.
As cold jewels enmassed.

Ruthless.
Raging.
Displeased yet clinging.
With ruminations attached.

I brace against their elemental anger.
Anger crushing my mortal self.
With damage intended.
But not administered.

The uninvited sharers of secrets.
Making me let out,

The mistakes gnawing,
And the shortcomings clawing,
Their known paths inside.

And the throbbing pains.

Everything has come back.
Every moment congealed into a darkling stab.
The haunters accost me this very instant.
Flames and flashes sprout and erupt,
Refusing to let go of my memories,
Scribbled and burnt deep.
Unlocking the vaults full of them,
Through my acts,
Reeking of imperfection.

All of you.
Family.
Friends.
Acquaintances.
Strangers.
Bulldozing your way into innocent lives.
Had never had anything to remind,
Save the drudgery and the sameness,
Of the life meant to be lived,
In the mellowed fires of reason and impulse,
Smouldering their cries.

And every moment this illusion rolls on.

Instances and everything that happened,
And is about to happen,
Will remind me of your monotony again.

You cannot take me.
I am already consumed.

You cannot outrun me.
I am in your arms only.

Incapable of peace and protests.

But I stay nonetheless.
The anguish meant to be lessened,
Gets buried even deeper.

And I stay.

And I live.

I fight the tried,

And the tested.

I have become mutiny.

I watch,
And witness my rebirth.
Inconsolable and desperate.

As the sun rays tiptoe their way back from me.
And the receding waves obliterate my footprints.
Never caring to remember them.

Don't Pull Me Back

Chunky squares of lights,
Winking back from the windows.
Miserable backs,
are hunched over study tables.
Exams to crush our souls the coming day.
Exams that bring hope of a certain afterlife,
Slightly better than this one.

This one's contents,
Already known to us.

Boisterous moments of revelry,
Calm ones of routine.
Boisterous ones were few and far between.
Calm ones were and are mandatory.

Exams won't crush our souls, I believed.
The absolutely vital piece of life called semester
exams.

But that was then.

Now, I still find myself underprepared.
Once again.
Dreaming the surmountable dread,

Of what I faced a few years back,
In college.

Did I say "face"?

Didn't actually dread it.
Few times they were events that got over soon.
Other times they took their time.

I dread them now.
Now that I have a degree and a job.

Panicky, punishing, nicotine-addled time.
Us knocking, banging on the numbered hostel
doors.

Beacons of stress,
High-strung with laptops and paper sheets.
Raiding someone's store of snacks.
No time to go and have dinner.

Still I went.

Dreaming it when wide awake.
I know that.
But it's not comforting in any way.
Not now also.

Someone daring or confident or both,

Or someone finished with the preparation.
But someone far away from me and my room,
Is blasting away music.
Speakers blare down the corridor with abandon.
I think it's Green Day.
Or Nickelback.
Not exactly sure what song it is.
Don't know what's up with him.

The music doesn't reach me well.
I have a feeling it will be diminished near my
room.
But I don't hope.
Don't want it to die when it nears my room.

I like what he has put on speakers.

I am still outside.
Walking back after a hasty meal.
To be a miserable back,
Hunched over my study table.
Flipping through course slides.
Poring over my notes.
Once again.

Upstairs lies the corridor.
A haunt of still air and suffocating serenity.
The music drags me closer.
Warms me,

And warns me,
To be more responsible and true to myself.
To think again,
Of the money parents put in for college.

I've unlocked the door of my room.
Don't wish to go inside.
There is no one there.

Or here.

Seems like brothers on the floor are past caring.
Not even a peep,
Or a door banging shut.

The night even rebels can't afford to revel in.

I am past all that now.
Don't have to sit for any exam.
Through all that came before,
I performed inconspicuous acts of sailing
through.

I am past all that now.
Now all that I do is try and walk back a little.
In my quiet moments.
Each new night.

Squarish chunks of lights,
Shining from the windows.
Miserable, hunched backs in the cold, still air.
Lighting up cigarettes,
Borrowed and their own.
Sipping stinging room-made coffee.
Chatting in the company of frayed nerves.
Not so looking forward to dawn.
Dawn brings the absolutely vital exam.

I am past all that now.
I pretend to think I am.
Like you pretend to care.
About me walking back onto,
The lanes preserved in my head.

Don't pull me back.
I won't make it.
I am stubborn and weak.

Not Past Longing

How about passing to a new life,
With the older ones' memories?
That way, you get to have it all.
The good, the bad and the ugly.

People don't stay with you their whole life.
Their memories do.

Memories wake up with you in the morning.
Some come to bed at night.
Some swish past your mind's eye.
When you are busy with day-to-day life.

Invisible, imperturbable bonds.
How do they get formed?
They do get formed.
You know that.
But how?

You like someone.
Someone likes you back.
You hate someone.
You get some of it back.

You ignore someone.

Someone thinks you are not even there.

You are born to someone.
Someone is born to you.

I know I should be past longing for someone.
Karmic touch got discontinued a long time back.
Conversations gone.
Voices gone.
Even some memories…
Gone.

Still,
Moments and faces remain.
A bit of this here.
A bit of that there.

In my halls of solitude,
I am not past longing.
Not entirely.

The Dream That Came True

I saw you in a dream.
After a long, very long time.
In that dream I could be said to be happy.
Outside that I didn't find myself to be.

It's a different face, but.
But I don't remember having seen her before.

Her laugh is there.
Not yours.
That was not your body either.
Maybe someone else's.

Still, I know it is you.
How come?

I don't know.

But that someone and I are having a good time.

In a restaurant.

Don't get any ideas.

A storm or earthquake hits the place.

Has us running here and there.

Trying to find a safe place.

In the morning, mom told me that an earthquake
did come in China.
That was an East Asian place in my dream!

What you woke up with that dream,
I get it.
I can work out the details.
Live with it.
Make it go to sleep.
But it's very hard not to feel it,
When it wakes up inside,
And tells you it's got you on the right spot.

Time for bed has come again.
Heart wants to sing but the hour is late.

Words wanted to gush out.
Have been wanting to for days.
Sometimes letting out some blood first,
Is the way wounds heal.

Or not.

I think I got drunk on that dream for far too long.
And now the dream is dead.

Words for Succour

Bedtime, boy.
It's bedtime.
What? You aren't sleepy?
But you slogged the whole day!
Aren't you tired?

I am.
I feel like I am tired of this question.
Aren't I tired?
I also am.
How many times has it been?
That you've asked me this?

Once again, I am being straight with you.
I am tired.
But I am not trapped at night.
The way I am trapped during the day.
There are hundreds of things.
Things that have to be done.
You know what I am talking about.
You know me too well, night.

Nights can be perfect, you know.
People log off for a solid amount of time.
Words stop being lazy and can fit perfectly too.
It's when I get some time to build my rhyme.

Nights can be repulsive too.
Like the one that's racking me right now.
Sometimes I do know you too well, night.
It's why I try not to get too close.
Best if you keep your secrets to yourself.
Well, some of them.

It's why I try not to get too close.

And yet now I can't get away.

That's why I have sought you out, words.
Will you save me from the clutches of the night,
That keeps asking me,
"Aren't you tired,
Of this whole charade?"
Of which I am a part.
Which has a role for me to play,
But not a happy one, I sense.

I have opened the window panes.
Feel the tug of the air outside.
It wants to whisk me away to someplace distant.
Someplace I don't know from scratch.
A place I would like to scratch.
Someplace free.
Where me and the wind are best chums,
And fly where we would like to.

And I bleed from the inside.

Safe in my home, safe with a job,
I bleed from the inside.

A Big Fraction of Bliss

Words can take over your life,
But only if you let them.
I have let them willingly.
And am willingly paying the price.

Supercilious freaks of mind.
Think they know it all.
Think they are the most important.
Ready to slay the ignorant.
Dazzle the inquisitive.
Or bore the bores.
And make them flee.

Words can take over your life.
Yet often they don't make homes for ever.
Nomads with their bivouacs,
They visit often if you are a friend.

After a long stay spanning weeks,
The camps have been struck.
What now?

What now?
The words you wanted.
They have left.

Emptied out of the cornucopia of your mind.
They departed without ringing it out.
Of its hollow present.
What now?

What now?
Did someone ask?
Or was it my own flickering voice?

Well, now would be the time,
For the bands to kick in.
With the guitars, the drums and the blistering
vocals.
And let me take a dip and a sip,
Inside and of their live hypethral brilliance.

The headphones slip on.
Or the speakers turn on.
Now that my supercilious friends are out of the
system.
I can afford to drift to some places I know I'll
like.

They can hide wherever they wish.
Go be friends with someone else.
Go cause a rift between friends.
Or go to sleep.
I think I am going to go again,
To look for them tomorrow.

The One I Chase With Eyes Shut

Running around.
Running around with my eyes shut.
Don't think I will lose my way.

I think I didn't.

But I tripped over something and fell.

Oh man, are these thorns?
Pressing deep and happily into,
My arms and my cheek.
Probing opportunistically,
My sides and my feet.

Scratches and stings.
Peeled-up skin and skin-deep pins.
Thorns alone to grab to free me up,
From new and all-too-familiar embraces.

Scene of a mock crucifixion.
Sheen of a mocking soul.
Shining through punctured limbs.
Gaping through unseen holes.

Grabbed hold of them thorns finally.
The sort no one else could.
Pulled the pain away.
Shorn of the 'pins and needles' at last.

Running around.
Running around in my mind.
Have put off looking for you.
My eyes are still shut.

Self-isolation is the Byword

They called, they talked,
They advised, they baulked.
Said I needed to be in good hands.
Hands that would keep me up and productive.

But they won't come here.
Can't come here.

They fear the virus.

My kids, they all left one day.
They said it won't get difficult.
That they would keep coming.

That wouldn't be possible, I knew.
Yet I let them go to their chosen places.
So the ones I sacrificed so much for have gone.
Closer to close friends and unknown faces.

It was bound to happen someday or the other.
I don't blame anyone.
Did the best I could.

How I wanted to be left alone sometimes,
When kids were still kids,

Didn't happen that way.
No time for me-time then.
Now when I don't want to be left alone,
There's plenty of time to be lonely.

With that neighbour of a virus,
Encoffining me alive.

I am cranky and old.
It's sad to admit.
Even with all the vigour and work and purpose.
Sad to admit that my bones have begun to ache
in the winters,
Even after having a heart that's far from being
cold.

The cook has disappeared.
Just like the neighbours.
I do can whip up the odd dish,
But the legs don't obey me sometimes.

He who lives alone is the strongest.
Losing that credo, I am.
I am beyond sorrow and trust, I like to believe.
But not pain.

A nagging fear follows me,
Like an unruly shadow.
Not sure if my legs will work tomorrow.

Printed in the USA
CPSIA information can be obtained
at www.ICGtesting.com
LVHW020047260124
769470LV00074B/2117